All About Your

Contents

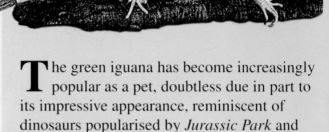

This five-year-old male measures 5ft – the tail makes up two-thirds of an iguana's length.

DID YOU KNOW?

Green iguanas are not always green. Many are shades of brown and orange, and some iguanas are even blue.

(ω) 639.395 N
0729111

T he green iguana has become increasingly popular as a pet, doubtless due in part to its impressive appearance, reminiscent of dinosaurs popularised by *Jurassic Park* and the *Lost World*.

With its dorsal crest of spines, long, powerful tail and discernable dewlap under the throat, the adult iguana is certainly an impressive sight.

It is also an impressive size, which is the biggest single problem facing most would-be owners. Before considering buying an iguana, you must be sure that you will be able to cope in a few years' time when the cute little lizard in the pet store has grown into a giant which could weigh up to 18 lbs and measure seven feet from head to tail!

Within a year you can expect your new pet to have reached two feet in length and by three years it will probably be well over three feet. It is essential that prospective owners fully understand that such a large creature will require expensive equipment and a very large cage to house it properly.

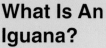

What Is An Iguana?

Iguanas are arboreal (tree-living) lizards. They come originally from Central and South America, their territory extending from Mexico to southern Brazil and Paraguay. They have also been artificially introduced to some parts of the United States, notably South Florida and Hawaii.

They are superbly adapted to life in the trees, using their strong, well-developed limbs and powerful claws. In their natural habitat much of their life would be spent high up in the canopy, usually in forested areas close to water. In times of danger, they have been known to drop from the tree in which they are resting into the water below to escape from predators. They are, in fact, superb swimmers, although there will be few chances to observe this behaviour in captivity, unless a very large enclosure can be provided!

Up to two-thirds of an iguana's length is taken up by the tail which, interestingly, can be shed as a defensive mechanism if the iguana is attacked. This behaviour is rarely seen in captivity but care should be taken with youngsters as they may react like this if grabbed by the tail. The tail, incidentally, does grow back, but will never be as attractive as the original.

The green, or common, iguana is a reptile and therefore is considered cold-blooded. The proper term for this is ectothermic, which means the animal derives its body heat from its surroundings, rather than producing heat internally as mammals do. This makes reptiles very efficient as they do not have to waste energy producing heat. Much of the food eaten by mammals, including man, goes into producing the energy required to keep themselves warm. So a reptile needs much less food than a similar-sized mammal.

In their countries of origin, iguanas form an important part of the economy as they are widely used as food, for producing leather, and they are also exported for the pet trade. Nowadays, iguanas are increasingly ranched commercially for these purposes, reducing the pressure on the wild population. However, iguanas are faced with a variety of problems in the wild, notably habitat destruction, which has led to a decline in both range and numbers of animals.

There is considerable variation in iguana colouring.

Understanding Iguanas

Iguanas should not be considered domesticated, in the way that cats and dogs are – they are wild animals. They are interesting to keep, but I would hesitate to call them pets in the true sense of the word. They are very similar to fish in this respect. Having said that, many iguana owners do develop a close relationship with their animals, letting them roam freely in the house or taking them out in the garden for exercise and access to sunlight. A range of custom leashes for this purpose is now available from reptile shops.

They make good pets for children and should encourage responsible pet ownership. They will not, however, interact with other family pets and should not be left alone with domestic pets, such as cats and dogs, which will make them feel threatened. Neither should they be kept with other reptile species whose needs would probably be very different.

Most iguanas will have been imported and may, understandably, be nervous at first. This is even more apparent when buying a newly-imported adult. Such animals will need time to settle into their new surroundings before they can be handled or let out of the cage.

On the plus side, iguanas:
• Are relatively undemanding.
• Do not need to be taken for walks.

Some owners develop a close relationship with their iguanas.

6

Think very carefully before taking on the responsibility of owning an iguana.

- Can be left unattended for short periods if the owner is away.
- Can be kept in homes where asthmatics are resident, as the lack of fur, feathers and their related dust makes them excellent pets for allergy sufferers.
- If properly maintained, are not prone to illness and require less maintenance than a dog or cat.

Could I look After An Iguana?

This is the most important question that you should ask yourself before you buy an iguana. Your animal will ultimately need a large living area and will be relatively expensive to care for. It is very important not to take on a baby iguana if you are unable, or not prepared, to look after it for its entire life. Zoos and animal rescue centres are burdened with many iguanas whose owners simply cannot cope with them when they get too large.

Remember, a baby iguana may cost no more than $10 to purchase, but the equipment you will need to house and care for it properly may cost a further $400.

With proper care, green iguanas can live ten to fifteen years in captivity. Over the last few years much has been learned about the requirements of these animals and we have seen great advances in equipment and product available for maintaining them. This is likely to prolong life expectancy.

Y ou can buy green iguanas from many pets shops, where experienced staff should be on hand to give you advice. If not, find another store.

What To Look For

Look for an iguana that is lively and alert. Make sure that it is plump and its eyes are bright, clear and round, with no discharge. Check carefully that it has all its digits and that its claws are unbroken and that there are no ticks or mites (see page 28). A young iguana should have a cheeky and inquisitive look and should occasionally flick its tongue as it moves about. Always try to choose an iguana that remains reasonably calm when picked up, as it will be easier to handle than a flighty or nervous animal. Iguanas store fat at the base of their tail, so this should be fat and rounded, with no bones visible.

Signs Of A Healthy Iguana

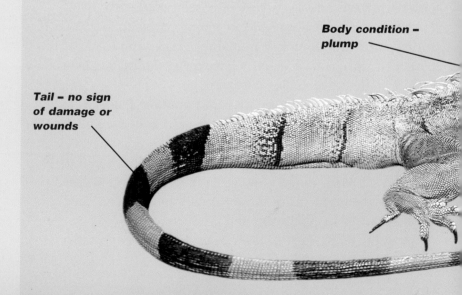

Body condition – plump

Tail – no sign of damage or wounds

What To Avoid

Do not buy any iguana that looks obviously sick, no matter how sorry you feel for it. Many people make this mistake, believing they will be able to nurse the animal back to health. This rarely happens. Instead you are left with large bills for veterinary treatment, disappointment, and a dead iguana.

Avoid any animals that:
• Appear thin and listless.
• Have prominent bones (particularly at the base of the tail).
• Have any lumps and bumps.
• Have swollen or missing digits.
• Have sunken eyes or a crust around the eyes. Sunken eyes are a sign of dehydration, and by the time this symptom is apparent survival is unlikely.

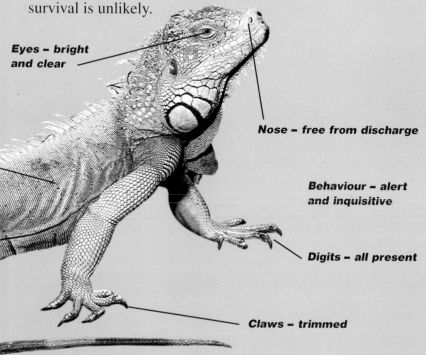

Eyes – bright and clear

Nose – free from discharge

Behaviour – alert and inquisitive

Digits – all present

Claws – trimmed

Some iguanas, particularly those recently imported, rub their noses on the front of the cage, leading to sores and abrasions. Animals showing such signs should be avoided, as they will probably prove nervous, could be difficult to handle and may well develop infections in any wounds.

It is also important to check the mouth and nose. Make sure there is no discharge, although a white salty deposit is okay, as iguanas excrete excess salt though their nostrils. The inside of the mouth should be pink and healthy-looking; avoid any animal with crusting, blood or fungal infection. Iguanas with mouth rot (see page 30) can be hard to treat.

Male Or Female?

Sexing young iguanas is an almost impossible task, although it may be possible to do so by counting the femoral pores on the underside of the hind legs. It will probably, therefore, be difficult to choose the sex of the animal you are buying.

In an older animal this is no problem; the differences will be apparent. Male iguanas are larger than females and look rather more impressive. They have longer dorsal spines, a larger dewlap, a broader head, very prominent femoral pores and may be more brightly-coloured. Females, on the other hand, will probably be less aggressive and make more tractable pets.

If you want to breed your animals, or simply keep a group, it is vital to know

The femoral pores on the male (above) are larger than on the female.

the sex. Two male iguanas rarely live together happily and will almost certainly fight in the mating season, particularly if one or more females are present. Groups of female animals will normally live together harmoniously. But even if females only are kept, they will still produce clutches of infertile eggs. Nesting sites must, therefore, be provided for all adult females to prevent problems with egg-binding (see page 30).

What Age?

It is always best to start with a young animal, between three and six months old, which will acclimatise well to its new life in captivity. If you do want a larger animal, choose one that has been in captivity for a long time. Some pet stores take in animals that have grown too large for their previous owners and, if you have the space, this is an excellent way of obtaining a sexable animal.

The size and the bright green coloration indicates that this is a young iguana.

Setting Up A Home

Y ou must set up your vivarium (the name given to houses for reptiles) **before** you acquire your pet. You will not be able to leave a young iguana in a cardboard box while you go about building it a cage.

Housing

Ready-made vivaria are available in a range of different materials. Glass fish tanks are really only suitable for short-term housing of baby iguanas and they will soon require a proper wooden or melamine vivarium, or one of the increasingly common moulded plastic vivaria.

The size of the vivarium will depend upon the size of iguana you have. A young pair may be housed in a vivarium measuring 36 x 18 x 18 inches (90 x 45 x 45 cms) and this will be suitable for the first year to eighteen months. If you choose a slightly larger vivarium (48 x 24 x 24 inches/120 x 60 x 60 cm) this will obviously serve as a home for longer. These starter vivaria are available from your reptile store. Most are constructed from melamine and have sliding glass doors at the front. If your cage has no ventilation, remember to drill a few holes (not large enough for the animal to escape through!) for this purpose.

This size of vivarium is suitable for a young iguana.

More living space is required as your iguana grows.

Personal Space

As your iguana grows it will be necessary to provide a much larger cage. The general rule is that the cage should be at least one-and-a-half times the body length of the animal in length, two-thirds the length in width and the same height as the length of the animal. Thus, for a five-foot (1.5 metre) animal, (easily attained in very few years) the cage would need to be 7ft 6in (2.27 metres) long, 3ft 6in (1.06 metre) wide and five feet (1.51 metre) high. Such a cage will need to be specially constructed, as few pet stores can provide a ready-built enclosure of such dimensions. Basic design would be a wooden box with sliding glass doors at the front.

Another option is to turn an entire room into an iguana enclosure, which is particularly suitable for breeding groups. Another way of providing housing is to utilise an alcove or storage area, blocking it in and installing glass doors for access. You could also use an old wardrobe or cupboard by removing existing doors and replacing with glass.

Keeping Iguanas Outside

In warmer parts of the USA and southern Europe, Iguanas can be kept outside for a large part of the time. Even in colder countries, like England, Iguanas will enjoy being able to get outside and bask in natural sunlight on warm days. A sturdy, aviary-like structure, with a wooden frame and wire mesh panels is probably the best and easiest to construct. The use of glass in outdoor enclosures should be restricted to small areas only, to prevent over-heating or burning. Concrete, brick and many other materials can all be utilised, and the size and complexity of your enclosure is restricted only by the size of your garden, your budget and your imagination. Alternatively, there are now a range of ready-made iguana-ariums, made from rubber-coated wire mesh, and these are ideal for those who are not so hot at D.I.Y. or for those who only want a temporary enclosure for occasional sun-bathing.

Heating

This is another important consideration as iguanas come from the tropics and need to be kept relatively warm. During the day the temperature should be 80-85 degrees Fahrenheit (26.6-29.4 degrees Centigrade) and this should be dropped to about 75F (23.8 C) at night. Adult iguanas can survive lower temperatures than babies (as low as 65F/18.3C can be tolerated), but babies should not be exposed to temperatures below 75F for the first eighteen months. Iguanas like to be able to bask under a spot lamp, which should produce a local temperature of 90-95F (32.2-35 C) and this should be switched on for six to eight hours a day.

The best way of heating the vivarium is by using ceramic heaters, or similar overhead heating systems. Undertank heaters and hot rocks are not really suitable for heating enclosures for iguanas as the areas involved are simply too large for these to be effective. These methods are also very unnatural ways for iguanas to warm themselves.

A reliable thermostat will be needed to control the heating element and

Maintaining the correct temperature is essential to your iguana's well-being.

prevent overheating. It is also a good idea to use a dimmer-type thermostat to control the basking lamp. All heating elements and bulbs must be protected so that the iguana cannot come into direct contact with the device.

Lighting

Special fluorescent light tubes are now available which are designed specifically for iguanas. These lights are called full-spectrum lamps, and they not only emit a high-quality light which will display the iguana to its best, but they also produce invisible ultra violet light. Iguanas, like many lizards, need access to UV-B light as this ultra-violet frequency is required for vitamin D3 synthesis. This is vital for the long-term health and well-being of your iguana. The tubes will need to be replaced approximately every year as the UV-B emission diminishes with time. The light needs to be on for approximately 12-14 hours a day.

Take care when positioning a heat-lamp.

The lamps must be placed in the correct position. The animal needs to bask close to the lamp to receive maximum benefit from the UV-B light and, ideally, the tube should be placed twelve inches from the basking branch.

Specially designed fluorescent light tubes are now available for iguanas.

Setting Up A Home

Cage Decoration

This is really a matter of personal choice, but certain conditions must be provided. At least one tree branch is needed for the animal to climb and bask on, and it is important that this branch is large enough for the iguana concerned. The branch should be fitted diagonally, from one side of the vivarium to the other, and should slope from the bottom to the top. It must be firmly secured so that it cannot fall and injure the iguana.

The floor of the vivarium needs to be covered with some form of substrate. You can use bark chips, wood chips, gravel, specially designed cage carpets or simply old newspaper. Whatever you choose to use, it is important that the substrate is regularly cleaned or replaced.

A tree branch is needed for the iguana to climb and bask on.

When you first take your iguana home it may be necessary to include a hide in the cage. This provides a retreat if the animal feels nervous, and can be removed once the iguana feels secure in its new home. You can also include decorative items such as plants. You could use live plants but they will probably be eaten by the iguanas or destroyed by their sharp claws so artificial plants are a better alternative. If you do choose live plants, make sure they are not toxic.

Artificial decor will stand up to your iguana's claws.

Water Bowl

You will also need a large water bowl for the animal to drink from and bathe in. Iguanas frequently defecate in their water bowl, so check regularly to make sure the water is clean at all times.

A large water bowl is required.

Handling Your Iguana

Learning to handle your iguana correctly is very important. Never simply grab the animal; always be gentle but firm, and make no sudden moves which could frighten it. Remember that iguanas can drop their tails, so never pick one up by the tail.

Tame iguanas can be encouraged to climb on to your arm but otherwise pick up your animal by firmly holding from above. Larger animals, or those which are not so tame, should be picked up using one hand behind the animal's neck and one at the base of the tail. Confidence is the key to proper handling and your animal will soon learn to respond to you.

Daily handling from a young age should ensure that your iguana becomes tame and used to you, but allow for a settling-in period for your pet to become confident in its new home.

Children should always be supervised by an adult when handling even young iguanas. Very large iguanas are best handled only by adults.

The correct way to hold an iguana.

Firm handling is required when your iguana is fully grown.

This form of restraint is required if your iguana requires any form of treatment.

Iguana Personalities

Like people, iguanas are all different. Some are outgoing and enjoy the company of humans, others do not. There is, unfortunately, no simple way to predict how any iguana will turn out. But it is better to avoid any babies that appear nervous.

Males are generally more aggressive than females but can still make excellent pets. Iguanas are generally not aggressive towards humans, but may occasionally be so towards each other.

Bites And Scratches

Iguana bites are not common, but they certainly can bite if provoked. Fortunately iguanas give plenty of warning when they are not happy, usually in the form of hissing and tail whipping. Failure to take heed of this could end with unpleasant results. While a baby or young iguana bite will be merely a painful nip, the bite from an adult iguana will be far more serious and may result in stitches being needed. Read the warning signs and this situation should never arise.

Scratches are by far the most common injury from pet iguanas. It must be remembered that iguanas are arboreal lizards and, as such, their claws are long and sharp to help them climb. If they become startled they will cling on wherever they are. If this happens to be your arm, you may get some unpleasant scratches.

Trimming the claws will reduce scratching (see page 24).

Iguanas have their own distinct personalities.

Feeding Your Iguana

Correct feeding is probably the most important aspect of keeping your iguana in good health, and is also the area in which most problems occur. Iguanas are herbivorous, that is they eat plants, but they will also devour insects and small rodents in the wild.

What To Feed

Young iguanas may eat insects but adults are generally totally herbivorous. Live insects, such as cricket and mealworms, are readily available from all pet stores which sell reptiles (and many that don't), and all of these are suitable for young iguanas. In the UK, locusts are also available.

Not all baby iguanas will eat insects, however, and they will thrive if fed exclusively on vegetable matter. The key to good diet is variety and it is very important not to let your iguana become fixated with one food item.

Mealworms.

Crickets.

Iguanas, particularly young animals which are growing fast, are prone to metabolic bone disease due to lack of calcium in their diet, so it is important to take this into account when feeding. Calcium-rich plant material should make up at least 35% of the diet and includes items such as greens, alfalfa, kale, dandelions (both flowers and leaves will be taken eagerly by iguanas), green beans and Chinese cabbage. Most lizards, including iguanas, require a 2:1 calcium/phosphorus ratio and, as many fruits and vegetables have a high phosphorus level, the calcium-rich items are doubly important.

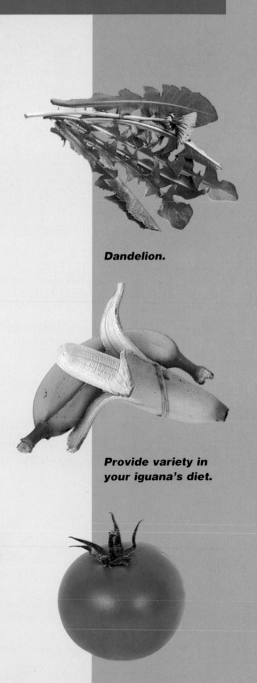

Dandelion.

Provide variety in your iguana's diet.

Most other fruits and vegetables will also be eaten by iguanas. Commonly used items include frozen mixed vegetables (thawed), carrots, bananas, tomatoes, grapes and lettuce. Experiment with as many different foods as possible to give your animals an interesting and varied diet. Members of the cabbage family should be fed sparingly as they can cause thyroid problems if given in large quantities.

Commercial iguana foods are now available but should make up no more than 15% of the total diet.

Feeding Your Iguana

DID YOU KNOW?

Iguanas cannot change their colour like chameleons but coloration and pattern will become more vivid under natural sunlight or broad-spectrum fluorescent light.

Feed your iguana as much as it can eat within an hour.

How Often To Feed

Young animals should be fed twice daily and adults can be reduced to daily feeding. Make sure food is of the correct consistency, that is finely chop all foods for young animals. Around two ounces of finely-chopped vegetable material should suffice for a baby iguana. If your animal finishes all its food quickly, increase the quantity, but if it leaves most of its food untouched, reduce the amount. If the iguana is growing and putting on weight, you have got the quantity right.

A good rule of thumb is to feed your iguana as much as it can eat in an hour and remove any uneaten items.

Water

Clean water must be available at all times. Most iguanas will drink from a bowl once they are used to it, but some might prefer drinking from a fine mist spray. This will also encourage healthy shedding and will be greatly appreciated by your iguana.

Vitamin Supplementation

Vitamin supplements are available for reptiles, and your pet store or veterinary surgeon will be able to advise on the best for you. Always follow the instructions provided and don't be tempted to exceed the suggested doses. Females should be given additional supplementation during the breeding season.

If you buy a good, healthy animal to start with, feeding should present no problems. The trick is to offer a varied diet and find out what your animal likes best.

Fresh water must always be available.

DID YOU KNOW?

The iguana's long, flattened tail is used as a rudder when swimming and also as a defence weapon. A lash from the tail would make any adversary think twice about taking on the iguana.

Caring For Your Iguana

Your iguana will appreciate being sprayed with water, particularly when it is shedding its skin.

Skin Care

Iguanas, like all reptiles, periodically shed their skins as they grow. Snakes do this in one piece, but iguana skin flakes off in patches. Occasionally skin does not come away properly, particularly on the toes, and any adhering pieces need to be removed. This is best done by spraying the affected area with tepid water.

Claws

Claws need to be trimmed regularly for the comfort of the owner as well as the reptile. This should be carried out on a regular basis and will

Ask an experienced iguana owner to help with claw-trimming.

require assistance. One person must hold the iguana firmly, while the other carries out the claw-trimming.

Clean the areas first, using a disinfectant designed for reptiles, then use sharp nail clippers to remove the end of the claw. Avoid cutting claws too short as you may cut into the blood vessals in the nail, which could lead to infection. Always ask advice from your pet store or veterinary surgeon if in any doubt.

The vivarium will need regular cleaning, and once a month the substrate should be replaced.

Routine Cleaning

Your iguana's water bowl and food container must be kept scrupulously clean. Faecal matter, uneaten food and dead skin should be removed from the cage on a regular basis and the substrate should be changed periodically.

The cage should be completely cleaned out at least once a month. Remove all furnishings and substrate and thoroughly clean the entire vivarium using a product designed for the purpose. Do not use a regular household cleaning product as there are a variety of vivarium cleaning products available. Cleaning glass in the vivarium will be a frequent task as iguanas do tend to make this quite dirty.

Going Away

Provided your equipment is properly maintained, your iguana will survive very well on its own for a couple of days if you go away. Do not worry about leaving extra food in the cage as iguanas, like most reptiles, can go without food for a comparatively long period. If you are going away for longer, you will need to make arrangements for the care of your pet. The best option is to ask a friend or neighbour to feed or check on your animal; if this is not possible, a number of shops now run a pet-sitting service.

The male iguana is likely to become aggressive when in pursuit of a female.

DID YOU KNOW?

Iguanas usually lay 20 to 24 eggs but can lay as many as 70.

Breeding iguanas in captivity is comparatively rare; not because it is difficult, but due to the large amount of space needed.

It is best to keep several females to one male, so that one animal does not have to bear his sole attention. Breeding male iguanas are single-minded in their determination to mate and will pursue females relentlessly. The prospective breeder should be aware of the fact that the male will also become very aggressive at this time and may injure, or occasionally kill, any rival that comes in his way.

Mating is a rather savage affair. The male grasps the female at the back of the neck with his teeth during copulation. The owner should ideally be on hand to ensure the female is not seriously injured in the process.

After mating, the female will gradually swell with the mass of eggs inside her. Iguanas usually lay 20 to 24 eggs which take 70-90 days to hatch at a temperature of 84-87F (28.8 - 30.5 C).

About three weeks before laying her eggs the female will stop feeding. This is the time to provide her with a nest site; a large box with a hole cut into the side is ideal. Potting compost or a sand and soil mix are suitable laying mediums. After laying, the eggs should be removed to an incubator until hatching, otherwise they are liable to be eaten.

Even if females have not been mated, they will need to be provided with a nesting site if it becomes apparent they are carrying eggs. Failure to do so could result in death from egg-binding (see page 30),

DID YOU KNOW?

Adult iguanas only normally grow to about five feet long but exceptional males may reach nearly seven feet (2.4 metres) and weigh up to eighteen pounds (8.16 kg).

It takes between 70 and 90 days for a female to hatch her eggs.

I f iguanas are kept in the correct manner, there should be little problem with disease. Most symptoms that arise will be caused by poor husbandry, particularly incorrect feeding. Watch for early signs that your animal is off colour. Things to look out for include loss of appetite, lethargy, swellings (both around the mouth and other body areas), difficulty in breathing or swollen digits.

External Parasites

Iguanas rarely suffer from external parasites and this would normally only be seen in newly-imported specimens. Ticks are the most common external parasite and can go unnoticed when they are small. The head is buried in the skin of the animal and the round, dark brown body protrudes above the surface. As the tick fills with blood, it increases in size and will be very easy to spot. Ticks can be gently picked off using tweezers, but ensure that the head is removed properly, or treated with a purpose-made medication.

Iguanas also occasionally pick up mites. Watch for unnatural rubbing against the side of the cage or branches. The mites (sometimes red in colour, sometimes black) can be seen scurrying on the surface of the skin of the affected animal. Mites can be treated with medication, but do use one specifically for reptiles and consult your vet or reptile store if unsure.

Internal Parasites

The most common internal parasite seen in
newly-imported reptiles is the nematode, or
roundworm. Many reptiles live perfectly
normal lives with quite heavy infestations of
this parasite, but in captive conditions, in close
proximity to faecal matter, they can become a
problem.

If your animal is eating well but losing
weight, or if there is blood in the faeces,
nematodes could well be the problem. Your
veterinary surgeon will be able to test for this
and treat the animal appropriately. The
symptoms described also apply to the other
common internal parasite, flagellate
protozoans. Again, if the problem is caught
early and treated promptly, your animal
should make a full recovery.

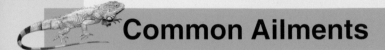

Egg Binding

This is probably the biggest killer of female iguanas. Being egg bound means she is unable to lay her eggs. This normally happens when a female has not been mated or has not been provided with a nest site. Typical symptoms are lethargy and a swollen stomach. This condition is very serious and requires immediate veterinary attention, often resulting in surgery to remove the eggs. Increasingly, vets recommend spaying female iguanas to prevent this condition.

Nutritional Disorders

Most disorders in captive reptiles are caused by poor nutrition, in particular calcium deficiency leading to metabolic bone disease. If you feed your animals correctly and have an appropriate full spectrum light tube, your iguana should flourish. Another nutritional disorder seen in iguanas is visceral gout caused by accumulations of urate crytals. Swellings in digits or limbs or small lumps on the body are typical symptoms.

This is usually caused by a diet which is too high in protein and is often seen in animals fed on excess animal matter, such as cat or dog food. Lack of water can also contribute.

Wounds

Your iguana may injure itself by rubbing its snout against the side or front of the cage. Wounds caused can become infected and lead to a condition commonly known as mouth rot. This normally happens because the cage is too small or the animal feels insecure. Consult your vet who will be able to administer the appropriate treatment. To prevent recurrence, ensure there are no rough surfaces in the cage and possibly cover part or all of the glass front until the wound has healed.

Health Warning

Iguanas, like many other animals, sometimes carry the *Salmonella* bacteria, and, on very rare occasions, this can be transmitted to humans. To eliminate this very small risk, a number of measures, which are largely common sense, should be adopted.

Never share food containers with iguanas (and that includes letting them eat off your plate – mad, but some people do it!), always wash your hands after handling your iguana or cleaning its vivarium, and don't use your washing-up sponge to clean your iguana's bowl.

Finally, however much you love your iguana, never kiss him...